My Daughter Is Drummer in
the Rock 'n Roll Band

My Daughter Is Drummer in
the Rock 'n Roll Band

Poems by Alexandrina Sergio

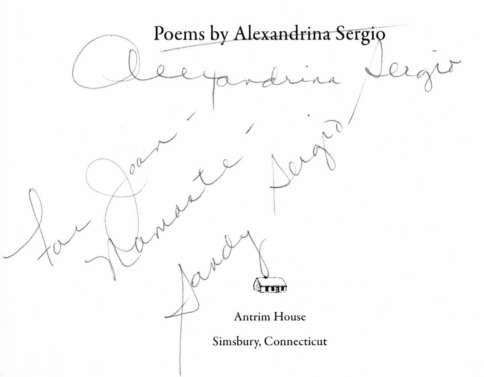

Antrim House

Simsbury, Connecticut

Library of Congress Control Number: 2009934530

ISBN: 978-0-9817883-8-8

Printed & bound by United Graphics, Inc.

First Edition, 2009

Photos of drums and drummer: Gillian Burdett

Photograph of author: David Sergio

Book design: Rennie McQuilkin

Antrim House
860.217.0023
AntrimHouse@comcast.net
www.AntrimHouseBooks.com
21 Goodrich Road, Simsbury, CT 06070

ACKNOWLEDGMENTS

My thanks to the editors of the following publications in which these poems have appeared, some in slightly different form:

Caduceus (Yale Medical Group): "All That Remains," "Aspergillum," "Memento," "The TIA"

Cold Shoulders & Evil Eyes... (online anthology, Universal Table): "I Never Know Whose Sister Is a Lesbian"

Connecticut River Review (CT Poetry Society): "Golden Wedding," "October Geraniums"

Double Lives, Reinvention and Those We Leave Behind (anthology, Wising Up Press): "Baby Of My Bones," "I Read of Your Death"

Encore 2009 (National Federation of State Poetry Societies): "Going In Style"

Long River Run (CT Poetry Society): "I Never Know Whose Sister Is a Lesbian," "Thanking the Lesser Known Poets," "In Search of a Suitable Demon"

Love After 70 (anthology, Wising Up Press): "Honoring My Mother," "Remembering Our Names," "Shopping for the Basics" (as "At The Supermarket: Shopping for the Basics")

Open Shutter (Thread City Poets): " Inner Ear Differences Found in Lesbians," "Sonnet to a Sonofabitch," "The House Told Me"

Wisdom of Our Mothers (anthology, Familia Books): "Forgiving My Mother"

Thanks also to the East Haddam Stage Company, whose actors performed the following poems in productions staged in 2004, 2005 and 2008: "Sonnet to a Sonofabitch," "Love Song of a Non-Singer," "The Company of Women," "The Sportsman."

The following awards are noted with gratitude:

Connecticut Senior Poetry Contest, 2007 (Connecticut Community Care), First Place: "When Wearing Purple Isn't Enough"

Dorman John Grace Poetry Contest, 2008 (National Federation of State Poetry Societies), Second Place: "Going In Style"

National Federation of State Poetry Societies Contests, Honorable Mention: "My Daughter Is Drummer in the Rock 'n Roll Band," "Marriage Baedecker"

Special Thanks

I am deeply—and affectionately—indebted to the Thread City Poets for their astute critiques and camaraderie. I also recognize the generosity of poetic guide and friend Alexander Taylor, sadly missed. Thanks as well to the Second Sunday Poets for their insight and wisdom. Heartfelt gratitude to Rennie McQuilkin, editor extraordinaire, for his artistry, skill and good-humored guidance. And for keeping me simultaneously grounded and aloft: Stephen Sergio, Gillian Burdett, Eric Burdett, Stacy Sergio, Lauren Sergio, Meg Gibson, Nathaniel Burdett, Lindsay Sergio, Alistair Sergio and David Sergio, life partner, first reader, music maker.

"There must be great audiences." Warm appreciation to Barbara Sergio and Pam Moran, Norm and Marilyn Gordon, Chuck Moushigian, Sona Moushigian, Susanna Moushigian, Ellen and Marty Abrams, and Pat and Don Luke.

for David, of course

TABLE OF CONTENTS

PROLOGUE

OLD LADY GONE BAD

TO DARE LOVE

ALL THAT REMAINS

...then laugh, leaning back in my arms
for life's not a paragraph
And death i think is no parenthesis

e. e. cummings

PROLOGUE

Inspiration in the Absence of Eyeglasses

Oh, for a Muse of Fire
Willliam Shakespeare, "Henry V"

Oh, for a Mouse of Fire!
Flames flicking from slick pinky ears
racing with smoldering tail
into the floorboard crack
to illuminate secrets to the poet sense.

MARAUDERS

Poems drop from the trees,
encircle my neck with their long skinny legs,
wrap my head with their spindly arms
then throw back their heads in teeth-shining cackles
of gleeful victory!

Some appear after rain,
translucent underfoot,
slimy and pervasive
in their flaccid presence.

Then there are those springing from godknowswhere
to cling, just out of sight, to my back,
clawing to surmount my shoulder,
snagging my favorite sweater,
making my stomach seize,
my breath draw sharp.
Long after they're gone
either forgotten or satisfied,
the red-thread scratches remain.

And, oh! the fragments.
Licking my face by the dawn's early light,
yipping to wake me from sleep in the night,
nosing my skirt and romancing my leg,
with shameless appeal sitting smartly to beg.

Some die and we bury them
deep in the wood,
marker crosses proclaiming
"This one was no good."

OLD LADY GONE BAD

Ring Ding Girl in a Linzertorte World

I dine on you as I would on madeleines: small smiling bites,
myself becoming as one with the melting Proustian crumbs.

I dab my lips with a linen napkin, its crisp folds hiding
that I was raised on Twinkies, Devil Dogs, Moon Pies.
Lots of them. In big mouthfuls,
my handy cuff the recipient of excess lard crème.
I wear ruffled sleeves and bracelets now
in case I forget.

MESSAGE TO A LITTLE BEACH GIRL

"I Want To Get Messy!" she shouts
racing to the tidal flats,
skidding to her knees in the oozing greasy black,
whooping with muddelight.

Take a roll in it for me, I say.
Go to it, Baby, I say.
Do it before it's too late, I say.

In Search of a Suitable Demon

*The happiness of most people...is not ruined by great catastrophes or fatal errors,
but by the repetition of slowly destructive little things.* – Ernest Dimnet

I envy those for whom
night monsters lie in wait.
No slavering beast crouches in the dust balls beneath my bed.
Rather, there is a mouse in my closet,
confirmed by peripheral sightings of tail tip.

A midnight horror keeps to his hairy ball until ready to spring.
The rodent, incessant, darting, chewing,
observes no such standards.
I spend nights huddled under covers,
shaking the quilts from beneath before daring the morning light.
I open the wardrobe door like a TV cop,
standing to the side to kick it wide.
I never slip my foot into a shoe
without first knocking it against the wall.
I hear scrabbling in otherwise silent pauses.

Nibbled to a quivering tatter,
I bargain with God:
Let me be ripped to shreds by a worthy opponent.

HONKY-TONK HEART

Truth to tell
I've never worn one of those
promise-filled, one-shouldered
blouses.

Never slipped my toes in and out of those
no-back, bad-girl
shoes.

But I can size up a fella,
calculate how I'd
unbutton his shirt,
button by button,
undo that silver buckle.

I think about it
just sittin' here in
my suburban skirt,
flippin' the pages of my
Book-of-the-Month.

You've read enough to know that
every Honky-Tonk Woman's got a heart.

I'm here to say that
every heart's got a
Honky-Tonk Woman.

YOU WILL BE NOTIFIED WHEN WE HAVE
LOCATED YOUR LUGGAGE

Trollop Underpants!
I know what they're up to,
dancing on the beach,
shameless beneath the Southern Cross,
flirting to catch the eye of a bongo player.

I never did trust those purple underwires.
There they go, surely, bouncing along the palm-brushed roadway,
waving at the shining men
who call out from passing trucks.

The shorts have no doubt run off
with a sailor shirt of no small charm,
consuming its sunburned face,
raking fingers through bleached-out hair,
rendering my careful packing futile.

The sandals, too, I know have dropped virtue at the threshold,
flinging themselves, one atop the other,
just beneath the edge of the bed,
keeping company with tracked sand, broken shells
and the trousers of an unnamed gentleman.

My travel outfit frowns and furrows its brow,
yearning to leave me naked in the airport
as it runs to catch the last wrongly routed suitcase out of town.

Message to a Young Woman

They sit sharing a book in Barnes & Noble,
hands touching briefly as if by mistake.
She wears an embroidered sweater.
He's all wire rims and tweed.
They dunk biscotti into cappuccino.

Oh sweetie, I do hope you'll end up with him
or someone like him:
someone who knows who Wordsworth was,
who can quote Toynbee;
someone who will like the men your girlfriends marry.

But before then
I wish you fried Twinkies,
a Saturday night at the car races
and at least one man who'll breathe into your neck
and call you Baby.

Spring Whirls into Town, Leaves Amazement in its Wake

The cardinal's call divides the sky
and on my window a sparrow taps and pecks
to get at his beloved,
so beautiful, so unreachable, shining to him beyond the glass.
Sudden heat after downpour has made the
hosta pips raise their bright heads, maple buds explode.
All my neighbors' lawns have magically unrolled from March
trimmed, fertilized, de-slugged to golf-green perfection,
except for Billie's yard,
where brown leaves and spiky odd grasses
are overrun by myrtle and phlox and daffodil
and violet and baby tulip,
unruly masses of pink, white, yellow, lavender, purple
jostling the cardinal, the crazy sparrow, my need
to sing loudly in the car
to let it be known that Spring Is Now.
Now!
Divide the sky!
Neighbors' lawns be damned!
Except for Billie's.

The Crack in the Driveway

My driveway has a crack in it and,
Alice-like, I slip down in
to the driveways of my youth,
which always had cracks
and tufts of grass spiking up to
impede the smartly regimented ants trailing to their
little sand houses on the edge.

My grown-up neighborhood features sweeps of ebony
to ease the way of homing motorcars seeking their
own tidy garages, not an insect villa in sight,

Up and down my street
the people villas all have doors of sturdy metal
embellished with curlicued scrolls or a single ornate initial
to tastefully suggest who might dwell therein.

The outer doors of my youth were slim and wooden,
with two screen panels,
and they slammed,
each resounding BAM followed by the dulled jangle
of the shuddering hook fastener.

Flies always seemed to buzzily dipdive inside during the
    pre-slam swing,
though sometimes they worked in through the
inevitable poked hole in the mesh.

My grown-up outer doors never slam:
they slooosh shut on pneumatic cylinders
and never admit flies,
which says little
because there are no flies anymore.

Where are the flies of yesteryear?
Maybe following after the old man whose
"Cash Paid for Rags" obbligatoed above
the Clop-Clop of his horse's hooves on the pavement.

Present Society admits no rags.
Garments are fated to live their synthetic-enriched lives
until ultimately, still serviceable but no longer fashionable,
they are deposited, whole-cloth, in the Salvation Army bin.

Gone, gone are the rags of my youth
along with the bread man, who,
to Mama's dismay and my delight would leave
unordered Danish pastry with the two loaves of white.

Ahh: the white bread of my childhood.
Tomato Sandwiches,
    Peanut Butter Sandwiches,
        Cucumber and Mayonnaise Sandwiches
filled the mouth with such exquisite melting sweetness.
Now there is barely a hint of sensual pleasure as the

schmear and the slices, rigid and fearful, sit
imprisoned on heart-healthy parched wholegrain.

I will fix the crack in the driveway,
so my neighbors will not curl their collective lip.

I will but very lightly patch over my yearning for
white bread and slammable doors
and an old man who'll pay for my rags,
should I somehow happen to have any.

BEAR MARKET

When my waist measured twenty-two inches
and glossy hair tumbled to my shoulders,
I would invest my yearnings in
Christophers or Gregorys or Kyles,
and, when available, the occasional Antonio.

I would write *Mrs.* and his name,
murmur it, fill my mouth with its consonants,
design towel monograms around it:
so much fragranced currency spent
on Jeffreys and Brads.

Only now, devalued in the weak dollar of less negotiable years,
do I see the folly of not diversifying,
of having discounted the Willys, the Johnny Lees, the Bears,
and, ever available, the frequent Bubba,
who would have left me, at least,
with some change to jangle in my pocket.

It's Like That

It's like finding a worm in your peach,
skirting its curved presence,
slicing the succulent fruit,
sliding it into a bowl.

It's like finding a worm in your peach,
carrying it with care on a glossy sliver
out to the veranda railing,
dropping creature and fruit over the edge.

It's like finding a worm in your peach,
using a napkin to lift it
between pincered fingers,
flinging it into the trash.

It's like finding a worm in your peach,
taking it between thumb and middle finger,
squashing it to spatters,
rinsing off the remains.

It's like finding a worm in your peach,
slipping it into an empty jam jar,
adding a bit of the fruit,
putting the jar on the table.

It's like that.

GOD'S IN THE RADIO

God's there in the radio
talking to you and me.
You ain't never gonna find him
by staring at the TV.

Now his radio of choice
is the one that's in your car
'cause that's where you get to thinking
that Hell can't be too far.

You're drivin' down the interstate
or on some muddy track,
all tense from peering through the fog,
aches creepin' up your back.

A friendly voice might ease the pain
so you twist the radio knob,
then scan through all the stations
for the one to do the job.

Then out He comes a-singing
about your lover lost,
about the pain you feel inside,
about its searing cost.

And whoever's vocalizing
you just know is channeling through

God's heavenly message, blessèd grace
and comfort meant for you.

Some'll say that you're just hearing
a redneck picker's story
but who's to limit where God's found
and how He shares His glory?

ASHES OF DEAD LOVERS

The urn came from Tuscany,
its swirls and flowers
suggesting yellow afternoon hills.
It is for storing the biscotti,
to keep the almond-studded spears dense,
firm enough to hold out against a
steaming bitter nemesis.

Some, of course, crumble,
leaving a grainy residue,
diamantine no more,
sweetness imperceptible.
She keeps them, nonetheless,
reminders of past delight.

Encounter with a Smile

When our grocery carts nearly crashed
in the melée that is Senior Discount Tuesday
his grin said
We're two of a kind, we're in this together.
In that instant
I knew how he had looked as a boy.

SHOPPING FOR THE BASICS

I like old guys with ponytails
and young ones lank and thin as rails
who ease on past the produce stands,
giant juice jars in both hands.

I do enjoy the dark-skinned youth
who flexes at the courtesy booth,
piercing eyes and high-boned cheek
like god both African and Greek.

I make my way by salad dressing,
smiling to myself, confessing
how nice again, at soda rack
to see the chap with hair tied back.

When no way can I grasp the bleach
stacked up so high beyond my reach,
I tell the gent who helps me out
he's shining knight without a doubt.

And when the bags are all packed in
by sweet old man with twinkling grin,
I head for home, hopes ratified:
this shopping trip has satisfied.

What? I forgot your damson jam?
Your pitted prunes? Your can of Spam?
Oh please forgive me, Dearest Love.
What could I have been thinking of?

Room of Rejected Kisses

Down a side corridor in the Hershey factory
is a room where a plump woman peels the foil from
inadequate candies and drops them into a bucket.

The sign on the door reads "Room of Rejected Kisses."

I'd give a year's pay for a room like that,
two year's, even, to get rid of the rebuffed sweets
that hover, dart, hit me in the eye at every turn.

IF I HAD TWO DEAD RATS

If I had two dead rats I'd give you one.
–caption, Bernard Kliban cartoon of a cat speaking to his beloved

If I had two dead rats I'd give you one
and make you a cup of tea.
I'd bring in the mail
so you could keep to your slippers,
curl around your back to make you safe at night.
I'd eat the stew that you would make for dinner,
let you wash and shine the windows,
weed the backyard garden
that you would know I need you.
And should the rat tail fall short of splendid,
please know that my intent was pure,
that perfect love is hard.

GOING IN STYLE

What sort of shoes to wear for a blind date
of unknown time and undetermined place?
I fear that backless bad-girl spikes would rate
attention that would but increase the pace.
I won't sport fuzzy slippers, pink and warm
(they'd be suggestive of an evening in)
or sequined platforms: too far from my norm.
The same for anything with soles too thin.
Perhaps stout hiking boots, their sturdy tread
resounding with a stomp of competence
to overcome the awkward social dread
that comes despite my call to common sense.
At end, I'll don steel toes for when we meet
in case his rusty scythe should scrape my feet.

Flying Trapeze School Next Right

road sign, Venice, Florida

If I appear in spangled tights could I get in?
Through all my years I have done well at sudden spin.
Incessantly I change my course right in mid-air,
have even done a loop or two, hung by my hair!

Where trouble meets my outstretched arms is when I fly
to grab onto the saving hand of spandexed guy
who I assume has put me on his must-do docket
only to find he's placed that hand into his pocket.

The thought pursues me like a clown car loaded full:
Is there a workshop with someone who's learned to pull
back from a soaring tumbler who can't seem to reach
quite far enough to swing one through a netless breach?

A seminar on timing might just take me far,
teach how to seize that hand before I leave the bar,
though mostly what I need to know in this regard
is how to tell when pocket lurks in leotard.

Sonnet to a Sonofabitch

Given a newfound plenitude of time
I study primitive war in savage cultures
and find some common themes in tribal man
reflecting grace inferior to most vultures.
Ritual defacement always played its part,
the sacred, the most treasured deep defiled,
and rape, of course, of any who were helpless:
the weakened man, the woman and the child.
So as I heap crushed relics in a mound,
visioning well-shaved cheeks smeared blunt with blue,
this microcosmic kinship with time gone
lends comfort of wry sort and brings the view
that as you stride your world with blow-dried gleam,
you're not the modern gentleman you seem.

The Sportsman

"This is win-win!" you'd crow, "just sport we seek!"
("Win-Win": you always used such jargon-speak.)
"We'll have the thrill of chase, of victory,
then loose the hooks, return them to the sea!"
"But won't it hurt and tear their mouths?" I'd ask,
not sure of how to do that crucial task.
"A bit," you'd say, "but God! It's just a fish!
Better a scar than parslied on a dish.
They do at end of day go free, you know.
It's not as though they're dealt a mortal blow."
Such games are in the past. You play no more.
You took your bait and pole and closed the door,
and time has almost healed the jagged rip
made by the barb embedded in my lip.

OLD MAN WALKING

He forwards himself
with the jut of vigorous old men,
shoulders hunched,
elbows bent,
head – bucket hat rammed down – thrust forward.
Joint and muscle tension
force his movement,
dare the wind to be in his way,
the same tension
that springs ago
pressed into the silken back
of any given partner,
insistence that
forced thighs too close
for good dancing,
that let her know
ballroom artistry
was not where he was going.

OLD LADY GONE BAD

I tell them that
if Jesus Christ should reappear
his message will be
For God's sake lighten up.

STAYING ALIVE

Should I awake to find my life's love gone
I'll shawl myself in widow's weeds,
eat plates of potatoes and simple meats,
read late into the morning's chill
and learn to tango.

In a Masonic Hall in another town
there'll be a master in silver moustache,
Astor Piazzolla in the tape machine.
In trumpet skirt and backless shoes I'll face
a youth too bored to live
or a sour old man with golden chains,
both but defining space for me.
My partner is the tango.

Brrum   dum-dum-dum
Brrum   dum-dum-dum
stirs memory of flutter in the loins
and I swirl with flames and with sunsets
and learn by heart and learn by heart
to stretch, to stride erect and bold,
move to side, elegance controlled.
Glide, glide, smooth aside.
Brrum   dum-dum-dum.
I learn to live the tango.

When Wearing Purple Isn't Enough

I

I want a hat
with stars suspended on spring wire
to bob around my face,
screen my big ears,
and make me look be-yoo-ti-ful
to the children who will point and say
"Oooh! See the Star Head Lady!"

II

I will arise and go now, and go to set them free.

I will step smartly along the sidewalk (avoiding the cracks)
stars swaying,
gathering the children
who will each one clutch on to the jacket ahead
to form a wavy worm behind me
until, with tiptoe touch,
upraised finger hushing the entourage-with-a-mission,
I'll ease open the
MAIN ENTRANCE
to the Brookside Convalescent Home
and the worm will wiggle through.

Our bottoms will graze the tiles as we crouch,
duck-waddling low past the desk

where the desk lady will blink to banish an eye speck
which somehow calls to mind
a peeking star.

Then away to the corridors!
I'll direct the gathering of the Geri-Chairs,
swaying stars signaling right and left, up and down.
The big boys will roll out the old men:
sleep-dressed once-weres
(still ares!)
with chins on chests, and rounded tummies
resting place for rumpled plaid shirts.

The little girls, in twos,
will flutter crocheted afghans
around the bent-stick shoulders of
almost-not-there ladies,
then station themselves on either side,
each dimpled hand carefully holding one of parchment.

When a chair-train has assembled
the stars will twirl.
GENTLECHIX! Start your Geri-Chairs!
and all the little feet in mary janes and Buster Browns
and Keds and junior trainers and Tevas-For-Kids
will launch from the non-slip mats,
bursting through the PLEASE USE MAIN ENTRANCE
to crazy-steer down the gravelly walkway,
across the (stop-look-listen) road
flinging through the surprised stone columns austerely

proclaiming CITY PARK 1923.
Rheumy eyes will open bright,
bald heads bob,
lap blankets furl with the gusts.

Twice or more about the rose beds they'll go,
careening past the swings,
angling by the concrete benches,
leaving a wake of gape-mouthed raised eyebrows,
only then to slow,
sneaking past the stern stone guards
to (stop-look-listen) cross,
    creak open the PLEASE USE MAIN ENTRANCE,
      slip in.
          Safe.

The big boys will lift the bemused flannel shirts
    onto narrow beds,
the little girls will pat and brush the yellowed wisps,
just in time for supper.
And even if there's no ice cream this time
no one will mind.

III

When the sky pales
and spikes its broom to drive the cowering leaves into fences,
I will button up (three buttons, one safety pin)
my shabby coat

and pull a wooly blue cap down over my star hat
so I will look too unimportant to notice or harm.

I will count out carfare, with perhaps a bit extra for a cup of hot tea,
and hurry for the bus in the November noon.
I will sit squarely in my cracked vinyl seat until just past
    Downtown,
to the neighborhood where pebbly buildings huddle close
    in the dust.

I will tread with care around crumpled brown bags and
    grazed bottles,
and bend to find a face in the heap of fusty coats beside the grate.
I'll whisper "Are you okay?" knowing the phlegmy answer will be
    a growl and a razor glare.
I'll pull a star from beneath my cap to press into the
    filth-rimmed hand
and drop another—a big one—down the grate
to perhaps deflect a bit more heat,
then be on my way before he decides to be afraid of me.

On the corner the youth huddled deep within his hood
will murmur "Some money, grandmother? For food?"
I have left at home the shawl of judgment I once wore with
    such flair.
I'll seek his eyes and pluck a star for that slim trembling hand
    to exchange
for cigarettes or liquor or drugs or whatever will give him a bit
    of comfort.
Someone more fashionable will tell him of the shelter
    and the meals and the program.

IV

I will keep my star hat on the double hook in the hall
with my shopping bag
and take them both to market.

Holding fast to the grocery cart, I will lean close to the jars
    of red-nosed olives
and strain to hear the hissing scraps of high-wire voice in the
next aisle:
"Bad girl...never take you again...no kitten" barely heard
through rising breath-caught sobs.
I'll straighten up and, stars dipping, briskly wheel around
    the bread rack
to slip a star into pudgy damp fingers and whisper
"You're a good girl."
Then I'll fold and shuffle on,
hoping that the streaky tot will save her star in a secret box
with empty spools and pieces of old jewelry
for her little girl to find.

V

When my star hat grows sparse
the breeze will stir it
and the few remaining bobbles
will catch the lift and carry me and my star hat
into the mist where it and I will be one,
suspended to glint, I do hope, on a dusky world
or maybe at least a few people in it.

TO DARE LOVE

HONORING MY MOTHER

I always park in the same place at the mall
to enter Macy's on a straight path to *Perfume*
where I pretend-study the offerings
and when unobserved
spray my wrists, behind my ears, even my coat,
mime a frown, inhale the back of my hand.

You played no such apologetic charade.
With panache you would make the rounds
to G. Fox, Brown Thompson, Sage-Allen, Steiger's;
lift glittering atomizers to your throat, hair;
fill the air with a delirious fragrance
that followed as you walked on to more mundane tasks.

Perfumers of the world would not approve your mix,
but a little girl thought you always smelled most wonderful.

I park in the same space,
head through the store
straight to you.

Forgiving My Mother

Because she loved me
my mother cut my sandwiches on the diagonal,
then cut again to make four little triangles on the plate.
Even for school day lunch she made dessert: cool easy-slip junket
or floating island, its meringue sail adrift on a sweet custardy sea.

Because she loved me
my mother protected me from deep water, dark places and
things that could cause me hurt.
I didn't play in parks or go to slumber parties or summer camp
or to any place where someone might not care enough.

I had no bicycle until I was twelve, first skated at sixteen
when a boyfriend took me on the ice, a different sort of virginity loss.
No rebel, I did not walk out past dark until eighteen.
Now grown attempts to ski or climb or swim display no grace
and only timidly have I dared the physical.

But I dare love, and do love well, I think,
because she cut my sandwiches on the diagonal.

Baby of My Bones

I

Baby of my bones
   and the bones of my mothers' mothers
   and the wasting bones of long-gone gray gone-frail mothers
whose breath rolls out
   to dare the world to harm the baby of our bones.

No place in my being is deep enough to hold you close enough,
baby of my soul,
baby of the soul of my mothers' mothers.

Child of my child.

II

In the time you were mine
   there was just you and me
   in one hour that was all time:
more precious than happiness,
   a gift of forever.

In the time you were mine
I heard the echoing whisper
   of all that was and is and is to be.

I touched your newborn hair still damp
   and brushed to kiss your tight-shut baby eyes

and beheld your wondrous baby fingers.

In the time you were mine
I told you things I knew.

An hour of all time was enough of all time
    because there was just you and me
and somewhere deep in you
    and in me
    lives the hour
    and all that is worth knowing.

III

The hour was gone and you were gone,
    taken to where other voices would hush the night sobs,
    other arms would stretch to draw the breathless,
    tippy first steps,
other hands would build the loom
    and show you how to weave the tapestry of your life,
    adding their own threads as well,
all but one bright strand,
    the very first
    laid down by just you and me.

IV

At every age
in every place
I see you.

Yesterday you were the beach baby,
    floppy white hat askew,
    crowing with delight at the extravagant legs of a hermit crab.

Tomorrow you will be the dust-streaked Little Leaguer,
    tossing cap to heaven,
    leaping and whooping in the glory of a Home Run.

Today you are the child in the park,
    belly laugh scattering to the sky,
    swinging with the unfettered joy of the immortal moment.

V

Children's laughter and Mothers' prayer,
with tidal swell and predawn drum and temple bell,
are one in earth's chant.

Your laughter and my prayer too,
child of my longing,

baby of my bones.

My Daughter Is
Drummer in the Rock 'n Roll Band

Burnished hair tossing to the pulsing light,
sticks hit and crash in their circling flight:
my daughter is drummer in the Rock 'n Roll band.

Hi-Hat clashing with the throaty bass growl,
left arm movin' like a panther on the prowl:
keeps 'em all together in the Rock 'n Roll band.

Five guys in boots sweatin' out their chords,
singer wailing blues striding up and down the boards,
all countin' on her rhythms in the Rock 'n Roll band.

Ran away from home when she was just twelve years ,
Left her Mamma crying for the grief and fears,
Never dreaming she'd be drummer in the Rock 'n Roll band.

Lost behind silence in her windowless space,
smoked pot, drank gin, sneered in Mamma's face,
then thought she'd be drummer in the Rock 'n Roll band.

Played drums in old garages and in barns choked with hay,
got good and then told Mamma to come and hear her play
when she got a job working with the Rock 'n Roll band.

Now her brother helps the sickly and big sister teaches school,
and the baby's doin' brain research, improving the gene pool,
while she's become drummer in the Rock 'n Roll band.

And their Mamma loves each one of them, as is a mother's part,
but somehow that redhead drummer reaches deep into her heart
when she triumphs over "Wipeout" in the Rock 'n Roll band.

At breaktime she'll find Mamma, flash a smile through barroom fug
and cross the room with arms outstretched in the exuberant hug
of an in-synch in-tune drummer in the Rock 'n Roll band.

Burnished hair tossing to the pulsing light.
My breath swells with tears at the wondrous sight
of my daughter, the drummer in the Rock 'n Roll band.

A Strange Land Has Come to Live in Them

After a long time their daughter comes home,
comes with a backpack, a sack of music,
and something unseen that slips with her through the doorway.

Though they had kept washrags and cleansers close to hand
they now barely notice
red tea splashes on tabletops,
crumbling grains of cake and rich breads
scattered across the counter.

At first they shuddered at the thumps
of dropped trays, heedless spoons,
but now those sounds seem the punctuation of ambient song.

They wonder how they had grown so circumspect,
so frugal,
as the shared cookie
gives way to heaping bowls of whipped confection
fragrant with almond.

They take a wider step
where they had moved with thrift.
They sometimes almost dance.

STACY THROUGH THE DOORWAY

The doorway
is like a cloud,

a dirty hanky cloud
that creeps across the summer sky
while you wait,
impatient for the sun to emerge
and bless your world.

The doorway is
any portal through which Stacy might stride:
the folding door of the Greyhound,
the entrance to a rendezvous restaurant,
the mouth of an airplane tunnel
disgorging bedraggled mommies with wailing babies,
grandmas and grandpas in Tilley hats,
lipsticked babes in leopard prints,
and, if all goes well,
Stacy.

Keen eyes and hard-life lines
tell tales unheard
what with the dazzle of blush and sparkle and glow
and I've-got-a-secret smile,
and the hair
tossed and tumbling,
red and brilliant.
Stacy is like the sun!

(Stacy is like the rain,
rain in its darkest muttering iteration,
rain that, no malice intended, stings and chills you
only because that's what rain does.)

So there you are:
fiddling with napkins and forks, or
stiffening your knees in the airport or
on a platform, wiggling fingers grown itchy
around the stems of wilting flowers
while you watch the conductor lowering
tots and handing down fragile ladies,

until...
Until like when from within a cloud comes the sun –
The Startling Flaring Warming Suffusing Sun –
Stacy Comes Through The Doorway.

Stacy comes through the doorway
and once again there is
Redemption
Salvation
and the world is warm
with the thrill of
Stacy Through The Doorway,
the thrill that happens every time
because
you're never really sure
that she'll appear.

When she doesn't,
it breaks your heart.

And when she does,
it breaks your heart.

INNER EAR DIFFERENCES FOUND IN LESBIANS

Hartford Courant headline, March 3, 1998

Because she has a Wonky Inner-Ear
my daughter loves women more than she loves men.

Her eighth vestibular otherwise seems
to send standard messages
about the slosh of earish fluids:

she doesn't fall over
or trip
or get cross-eyed dizzy.

Maybe her feet—big for a little lady—
keep her from tipping,
keep her grounded

So that she loves the world
        loves life
        loves children
        loves truth
        loves learning
        loves beauty and
        loves women.

Is the lesson that if you have a
Wonky Inner-Ear
you'd best have big feet?

I Never Know Whose Sister Is A Lesbian

until I put on the perky face,
babble about how my new
grandbaby has two mommies
and isn't it wonderful.

I hear the muttered "lesbians should have cats,"
don't miss the tight lips, the averted look
indicating that the miracle of a child's birth
is only wondrous when the sperm is delivered
direct.
By an identifiable male.
Even one who has made but a cameo appearance
    in the backseat of a Ford Escort.

More often than you'd think, though,
someone murmurs
"My sister's a lesbian, you know."
And then, released, we revel in
life entrusted to our hands,
a donor's gift,
bravery,
hope,
the spring that keeps its promise every time,
despite tight lips.

Near Encounter with a Queen

I didn't say "Hello. Great shoes."

An arresting presence in the Goodwill:
blossomed cloche captured blond curls,
slinky skirt defined narrow hips,
caressed lily-stem legs.

I didn't say "Hello. Striking hat."

Draped in unsettling sexuality
she strolled jeweled belts, sheer blouses,
picked, viewed,
Adam's apple constricted, jaw squared.

I didn't say "Hello. Finding anything good?"

Exotic flowers must be cultivated
should they dare to grace
the nodding predictability of
suburban gardens.

I wish I'd said "Hello."

The Company of Women

Oh! The Company of Women
is pillowed by burgundy velvet
and laughing deep from unselfconscious belly.
The Company of Women
is audience to the sisters' song,
is all delighting in what delights one,
is knowing forgiveness.

But then...but then...
I do like men,
their bodies blocking the windy sting,
their approval warming with the sun of long-ago fathers.
I do like men,
the rough of stubble and
brotherhood's lingering badge of sweat and smoke
giving reassurance in the dark.

And still...in the Company of Women,
hating what hates the other,
touching with assurance,
the listening and hearing satisfy
like the swirl of wine on the tongue.

But then...but then...

When so much of life is slashed by win or lose,
what luxury that there's no need to choose.

BIKE RIDE

In my perfect life I would wheel with you,
three speeds at my command
on country roads
with cows and flowers and dusty tractor trails
and the occasional breathless swoop
of hillside adventure.

In the existence where I sweat,
I slip off gingerly to push up the hills.
Should you turn and catch me in dismount
I mutter something like
"I think the derailleur needs to be torqued down,"
and you pedal on, satisfied.

You gift me with ten, then fifteen,
then twenty-one speeds:
breathless marvels of discouraging encouragement,
which leave me mystified and panting
and paralyzed,
as you ride on ahead.

How many cool days of cows and flowers and hillswoops
could we ride together
if I didn't always have to torque down my derailleur,
if I knew what a derailleur was,
if I weren't so unworthy
of love that requires torquing down.

PROPOSAL FOR A JOURNEY BENEATH THE SUN

I know the signal to make the camel fold his bony legs.
When he does, climb onto the seat.
Don't put your hand near his eyes or mouth:
camels can be quite nasty.
Give our steed a little rap
to make him move.

Your burnoose will swirl about you,
the sand glow yellow,
pools shimmer just out of reach.
Distant whirls will leap from the horizon to climb the sky.
The ride will jog you, bumping your innards.
The ungainly animal will sneer at your dependence.
Sometimes the grit will crumble under your eyelids,
your throat will crack dry.
Sometimes you'll nod, lulled by the undulating ride.
When the beast's gallop belies his awkward promise,
your laugh will tumble in the wind.

Then the Oasis.
We'll slip down,
drink deep,
eat dates,
kiss,
raise our orange tent,
lie entwined in wooly shawls.
We'll praise the humped, homely, unpleasant camel.
He is the only way to make this journey.
I hope you think it worth the doing.
I hope you know the burnoose becomes you.

Being Montreal

Montreal!

Where Notre Dame's wild rebounding bells
seize the body,
overtake the spirit,
make me one with their echo,
make me one with Montreal.

If I were Montreal
you would be
the west end of St. Catherine Street,
stepping out in improbable heels and fashionable trousers;
you would be black-garbed St. Denis in a geometric scarf,
sipping sidewalk coffee from a small mug,
nibbling a croissant.

I lack the grit to be Chicago,
don't care to be many-armed New York,
to be Paris or even Boston would be to pretend,
but Montreal!

If I were Montreal
you would be
the singer and the song
filling the soft moonlight of Parc St. Louis,
the juggler and his towering unicycle
fascinating the attention of Prince Arthur strollers.

You would give your passion, sure of its return,
if I were Montreal.

ISLAND AFTERNOON

You smile, murmur: *So this is why*
we came to this sunlit place?
The tufted spread makes creases on our arms and faces
in the island afternoon.

We barely sense that a bird has darted in one window
    and out the other,
not even pausing in his yellow flight to judge the drowsing two
who could right now be handling bright fabrics or turning
    African dolls
at the dockside stalls.

The mountain switchbacks deliver up the exertions
    of canopied taxis
crammed with swimmers clutching totes and towels and goggles,
adventurers prepared to leap down at road's end
to become one with the bluegreen waves.

Echoes of unassertive construction make chorus with the island dogs,
daytime roosters answer bleating goats
and crisscrossing all, the rumble of motor launches
taking bearded Englishmen back to their tall masts.

You stir, touch me,
and it's enough to know that
the astonishing harbor with its amazing sails,
the transparent sea gleaming with blue-striped fish,
the rum punch at the beach bar
and even the marketplace vendors in their brilliant crocheted caps,
await below, ready for us whenever we arise
this island afternoon.

MARRIAGE BAEDEKER

Travel in the country of your choice,
but not in one you've read all about
or that your friends visited.
The trip will not be a vacation.
Don't demand ham and martinis
but be a brave adventurer
with no cherished expectations.

Pack light.
If you need a safari hat or sandals
you can pick them up along the way.
List in your travel journal the places
where you find delight,
noting but briefly the towns you won't revisit.
Make sure not to get so wrapped up in the forest
that you miss the breathtaking endless lake.

GOLDEN WEDDING

Not for me,
getting dressed up, going to church,
repeating wedding vows.
It's way too late to be re-promising,
re-telling what we'd each start doing
to make blissful the life of the other.

More likely we should vow to stop doing.

You could pledge to stop leaving pot covers unwashed,
hoarding old concert programs,
drinking more than one martini.
I might swear to forgo the equatorial thermostat,
the cheery lights in unused rooms,
the flourish of the late arrival.

What use to alter such things now?

My promises give way to prayer,
prayer that I will never awake
to a day without you in it.

LOVE SONG OF A NON-SINGER

When we sleep apart,
my world's too wide,
and with night's whispered sense as guide
I tread barefoot to your bedside
to hear you breathe.

Morning Deer

If you were not here
who would care that I saw two deer
in the morning light?

ALL THAT REMAINS

ARS POETICA: A WARNING

Be careful what you write.
Someone might feel it.

She stopped me in the stairwell
to say that Fate
or her dead grandmother

had directed her to come
to this unaccustomed place
to sit with the poem writers.

She said my poem was her story,
one she thought no one could understand,
until this night.

She cried, grasped my hand,
never came again
to sit with the poem writers.

THANKING THE LESSER KNOWN POETS

I most enjoy the programs
where people read their favorite poems.

When they finally ask me to read
I will read the gift words of my friends,
poets who will be surprised that I have stored their lines
where I can frequently lift them out
to rub against my cheek, hold like a beach treasure to my ear.
I'll tell the poem of the high school chum fifty years ago
who wrote that her brilliant world turned into mocking pastels
when her lover left,
But I'm a winner just the same;
My life was gray before you came.

Sometimes words have vanished
but I still hold the pictures:
a pal's wet footprints trailing her on the tile
as she walked into Liz's house after a swim,
the screeching greasy crows despised by Shayna...
Sometimes the poet is one with the poem, and I recite
the sweet comfortable woman
silhouetted before me on the path, holding hands with her husband
who has come to take her home after she read a poem about her son,
her boy who now lives in starlight and shines on her.

IMMIGRANT

"In Bulgaria I'm a different person."

The houses and birdbaths,
the trees, the people,
are all images on boards.
Menace stirs behind every stage-scene fence.
I am ecstatic when the dog proves tied.

The sun's scorch blinds me to the road.
I tread like someone with a dropped foot,
grazing down to detect ruts and stones.

The men, the women, the children...
(Such straight teeth! Such magazine clothes!)
I capture and tame the words they sing.
Their tunes and rhythms escape.
My lyrics clash with the music,
halt the room like an elbow on piano keys.

The mirrored face is vaguely familiar.
I've become a slice of me.
I'm not sure which slice it is.

OCTOBER GERANIUMS

His new wife, she's heard, runs marathons.

We pull up summer plants still in bloom,
replace them with brilliant oranges and yellows
destined to crumble brown at first frost.
October geraniums explode
with the shining desperation of the once-favored,
exert to be noticed, to not be discarded
in favor of something deemed more in season,
something whose time in the sunshine has come
though theirs has not yet gone.

MEMENTO

I prowled her old back yard, peered into empty windows,
pulled defeated flowers from the planter box.
A spoon lay in the driveway,
fallen from the truck that had carted her things to the dump.
(Junk. Nothing to bother saving or giving:
mismatched plates, souvenirs, kitchen silver.)
I picked it up, wiped it clean with my glove,
brought it home.

The spoon is gently curved, its luster soft
through the fine abrasion that some cherish as patina.
I riffle through the drawer to find it for my morning cereal,
again for the cups of tea that punctuate my day.
It balances lightly on my fingers.
I contemplate bringing it to her when I visit,
fear she would ask what they have done with the rest of her life.

THE HOUSE TOLD ME

The house told me before he did,
a message from the empty stare of windows,
the gardens gone clumsy.

Still, I didn't really know.
The neighbors wondered, too,
but he dashed by in irregular pattern
and couldn't be captured.

Then I caught him one late night,
myself in irregular pattern, walking a guest's dog.
I cornered him at the hedge
where he had paused to lean on the dark.

It wasn't hard to speak in the shadows,
with a silky little dog for distraction.

"Is it true," I asked,
"what your house is telling?"

"It's true," he said.
"She's gone."

EARLY SNOW

It's too soon for snow
yet it falls with the leaves,
both touching rimy ground
on the same breath.

> *The cancer grew,*
> *even as the fresh life.*

They scattered her ashes today.
The baby whimpered in the cold,
ruffled the withered leaves,
stuck out her tongue to taste the snow.

The Comforters

"You should get a dog."

Pained brows gather around
to touch her shoulder and deal advice from tote bags.
Her arms overflow with the offerings.
Her tissue paper response barely disturbs the animated sympathizing.

"Everywhere I go he isn't there."

I Read of Your Death

Young years ago
I refused you.

Now appears something
like an eggshell,
a puzzling thing
broken open,
empty,
its fragile inner skin
twisted into strings.

The story I read
is that of a stranger
with your name
who journeyed beyond
what I ever knew,
upon whose dying
I discover
part of me
I didn't know was there,
part of me
I couldn't know would break.

Morning Papers

She pencils in the easy answers
and catches herself asking about a 20's actress
or a five letter verb,
her words fading
in the incomplete exercise.

She dusts the books
and rinses the few dishes
while his shadow rocks in the corner.
If she doesn't look
she can see him.

She wears his jacket to dig in the flower beds,
tugging the collars close around her face
when the wind stirs.
Safe within his outdoor smell,
she stays planting even when the bats have begun to dart.

At night she reads
until the book slips down into heaped pillows.
At light she brings in the papers.
Every day new headlines.
Every day the same news.

REMEMBERING OUR NAMES

I chide him for keeping the battered old rolodex.
"Most everyone in it is dead or gone,"
I tell him, "and besides, it's too big."

I reach to put it with the trash
but he opens it and reads the names out:
Queenie,
Mary,
Joe,
good neighbors long moved on.
Uncle George,
Aunt Kate,
Ken, my dear funny cousin,
Lois,
dead, all, for years.
Pete,
Ron,
Ellie,
friends absorbed by time and distance.

I put the rolodex back on the shelf,
each well-fingered card
a record of love,
a faded piece of the puzzle
of who we are.

Death Is...

It comes not little on cat feet
nor is it noble foe.
It's less than dying of the light,
it surely is not a good night,
it's pasty, stooped and low.

It faintly smells of unwashed things
and sponges too long kept.
Its poetry is off the mark,
its aspect grimy more than stark.
It's styleless and inept.

The priests and poets ask us to
conceive death as a force.
It's more a fact of nature's whim
like mildew on the toilet rim,
unworthy of discourse.

All that Remains

After Tante Betty died
the nephews came in Oliver's mustard-colored pickup
to take away her things.
The furniture and dishes were left for the renters
but the boys put old sheets down in the truck bed
to protect the bright fabrics brought from her stall in the market.
All the same broad, fringed cut,
they were beach skirts for the young girls, sarongs for the women,
and for the gray-haired ladies
Tante Betty would drape the flowered lengths on frail shoulders
and advise, "For de night breezes. So pretty."

The nephews took them back home and passed them out to
the mothers, first, then the sisters and girlfriends, then the
   cousins and teen-aged daughters.
Some were wrapped around slim bodies; others were hung on
   the cement walls of this or that island house.
One was held close by a girl
who brushed her cheek against the soft pink and lavender.

Now We Are The Aunts

They were always there, The Aunts,
side by side
like fieldstones crafted into walls by country artisans,
one piece coupled upon its other,
gaps filled by stones of chosen shape,
mortar scorned
so that when spring rains pound,
the rocks give up seepage and the flood works through.
Such walls hold cache for childhood secret,
lover's message,
invite meadow lunches
and sunshine rest,
are always there
though some stones ease out and are replaced.

Sister in Winter

I

Through sparkling fresh drifts
we hold hands and tread the snow.
Big and small footprints.

II

Tumbled angel wings
decorate the paths we make.
Snowmelt in the sun.

III

Hugging to keep warm
she looks back at the footprints.
So far from our home.

IV

I sense winter chill
overtaking her spirit.
Will buds bloom in spring?

ASPERGILLUM

"They sprayed holy water on the bikes and the bikers
with their aspergillums, the metal [shakers] that are
dipped into vessels of holy water."

Hartford Courant, May 24, 2008

The priests and deacons
whirl their aspergillums,
bless the bikes,
shower each gleaming machine,
each studded rider
with prosperities of
Clear Sky,
Smooth Road,
Safe Journey.

Were I allowed an aspergillum
I would leap, dance it about you,
command its baptism to inundate you
with remembrance of
teen boys who whistled when you walked by,
your fold-out honeymoon apartment,
a first paycheck red coat,
what you had for lunch,
who visited today,
my name.

This denied,
I would bend, fold my hands,
beg the waters at least to touch you

with gentle fortunes of
Clear Sky,
Smooth Road,
Safe Journey.

My Sister's Wings

My sister's wings are enclosing her,
pressing her shrinking core.
Thinning, stringy, they no longer support exuberant journeys.

Once eagle wings swept her aloft,
flapped and beat to protect the fledglings,
spread wide in welcome and respite, sheltered and comforted.

My sister's wings are flightless now,
a narrowing cage,
at once sparse and unrelenting.

I try stroking the fragile wisps
to awaken in her limbs remembrance
of when she sought the sun.

I tremble, knowing that her flight has cut the air for mine,
that as her wings cease to lift
I no longer soar.

I Tell Her

about the houses she's lived in,
her wedding,
the funny things,
the old political people
we once gleefully skewered
with the sarcasm learned from our Irish mother.
She smiles at the tales—
they're not like how most talk at her,
always quizzing,
saying "You must remember."
She doesn't, but she still knows how to feel stupid
so she says "Oh yes, I remember."
I tell her about the snazzy royal blue suit
with nailhead arrows across the front,
better looking than it sounds,
tell about the beach days,
the red two-piece that turned the guys' heads,
and she listens, sometimes looks surprised,
says "I love your memory."

She's being wisped away as if on indrawn breath,
more there than here.
I scramble to gather up the pieces she's dropped,
give them back to her,
but when she turns
she takes only stories.

Late Day Walking

The dark Hudson moves deep,
grainy ice riding eddies downstream,
gray fern shore dappling its surface.
I make a little game on the riverside pathway,
try to match my footsteps
with the prints I made going out.
When three snowmobiles rumble by,
the last of the gleaming masked riders
waves to me and I wave back, smiling,
warmed by such a greeting in February chill.
A pale snow moon hangs ahead in the late day sky.
I walk on toward it,
the smile still playing on my lips.

Early April, Warrensburg, New York

The ice cover has shattered on the Hudson
whose swift current becomes both master and servant
to the floes that ride the spring river downstream,
unimpeded by the clamor of swirling eddies.

At river edge the broken slabs rush to the banks,
scour away wiry shrubs and saplings,
leave behind a fragile ice meadow
to cradle the astonishing first wildflowers.

Old tales tell of Eskimo elders wrapped in wooly skins
set out upon the floes to make the voyage to eternity,
and I think perhaps this might not be the worst way
to make that journey.

THE T.I.A.

T.I.A.: Transient Ischemic Attack, or "mini-stroke"

I'm going to die someday.
I didn't know that until last week
when the T.I.A. delivered its clotted message
while I was otherwise engaged.

Barring fall from an oceanside cliff,
this, then, gives some promise
of how—and that—I will die.

The T.I.A. with its pigeon-toed eyes and speechless leg
arrived on the interstate amidst thundering tractor trailers,
a respectable place for me to be at the time.

But next time?
(And there will surely be a next time.)

Dear God,
let it not be in the Wal-Mart;
Nordstrom would be fine, or Lord and Taylor.
Let its visit not find me watching Magnum P.I. reruns.
Rather, let the world note that she was taken while dancing,
laughing at table with her children,
enfolded in the embrace of one she loved,
or at least shopping in someplace classy.

About the Author

Alexandrina Sergio traces her passion for poetry to her Irish mother's habit of mixing in the works of Celtic poets with bedtime nursery tales. William Butler Yeats and Little Red Riding Hood equally inhabited her childhood. As an English teacher, Sandy coached prize-winning student poets. Subsequent careers as executive director of a community-based mental health agency, director of a philanthropic foundation, and consultant in philanthropy encroached on poetry-writing time, but retirement has allowed broader opportunities for writing and reading her poetry. Her work has been published in a number of journals and anthologies and has twice been performed by a professional stage company. Her awards include first place in the 2007 Connecticut Senior Poetry Contest and second place in the 2008 Dorman John Grace Contest. She lights up at the sight of a microphone. Sandy and her husband, musician David Sergio, have four children and three grandchildren. They live in Glastonbury, Connecticut.

This book is set in Garamond Premier Pro, which had its genesis in 1988 when type-designer Robert Slimbach visited the Plantin-Moretus Museum in Antwerp, Belgium, to study its collection of Claude Garamond's metal punches and typefaces. During the mid-fifteen hundreds, Garamond — a Parisian punch-cutter — produced a refined array of book types that combined an unprecedented degree of balance and elegance, for centuries standing as the pinnacle of beauty and practicality in type-founding. Slimbach has created an entirely new interpretation based on Garamond's designs and on comparable italics cut by Robert Granjon, Garamond's contemporary.

To order additional copies of this book
or other Antrim House titles, contact the publisher at

Antrim House
21 Goodrich Rd., Simsbury, CT 06070
860.217.0023, AntrimHouse@comcast.net
or the house website (www.AntrimHouseBooks.com).

•

On the house website
are sample poems, upcoming events,
and a "seminar room" featuring supplemental biography,
notes, images. reviews, poems, and
writing suggestions.